Building the Shining City

The Grassroots Lobbying Guide for Christian Activists

A CHRISTIAN VOICE HANDBOOK
FOR RECLAIMING AMERICA

Cover design by John Connors.

Books are available at special discounts for bulk purchases from the publisher. To order, please use the coupon on the last page of this book.

Christian Voice is incorporated under the IRS code as a 501(c)(4) nonprofit corporation. Christian Voice, established in 1978 as a national lobby and educational organization, researches issues and legislation important to the religious, moral, and pro-family values of the United States, and disseminates this information to interested American citizens.

Printed in the United States of America

ISBN 0-9721535-0-0

10 9 8 7 6 5 4 3 2 / 10 03

Acknowledgements

Many thanks and God's blessing to Gary Jarmin and the other concerned Christians who, coming together from all walks of life, helped develop the strategies for reclaiming America.

And the deepest appreciation to one of God's finest, the late Dr. Bill Bright, founder of the Campus Crusade for Christ ministry, for his permission to include material based on his excellent work, "Your Five Duties as a Christian" as the first chapter if this book.

"Ye are the light of the world. A city that is set on a hill cannot be hid. Neither do men light a candle, and put it under a bushel, but on a candlestick; and it giveth light unto all that are in the house. Let your light so shine before men, that they may see your good works, and glorify your Father which is in heaven."

—Matthew 5:13-16

"We will be as a city upon a hill. The eyes of all people are upon us, so that if we deal falsely with our God in this work we have undertaken and so cause Him to withdraw His present help from us, we shall be made a story and a byword throughout the world."

—John Winthrop, 1630, seeing the Massachusetts coast from the deck of the Arabella

"Two hundred years ago Tom Paine, when the thirteen tiny colonies were trying to become a nation, said we have it in our power to begin the world over again. . . . Together we can begin the world over again. We can meet our destiny and that destiny can build a land here that will be for all mankind a shining city on a hill. I think we ought to get at it."

—Ronald Reagan, September 1980

"I've spoken of the shining city all my political life, but I don't know if I ever quite communicated what I saw when I said it. But in my mind it was a tall, proud city built on rocks stronger than oceans, windswept, God-blessed, and teeming with people of all kinds living in harmony and peace; a city with free ports that hummed with commerce and creativity. And if there had to be city walls, the walls had doors and the doors were open to anyone with the will and the heart to get here. That's how I saw it, and see it still."

—President Reagan's Farewell Address, 1989

TABLE OF CONTENTS

FOREWARD

By Rev. Robert G. Grant, Ph.D.

Amerca's roots are deeply planted in the spiritual legacy of those pilgrims and early forefathers who established this nation "under God." They were, almost to a man, professing Christians who came to America in search of freedom: of a place where they could raise their families and worship God in the church of their choice — free from the interference of a hostile state.

With just one exception, the signers of the American Constitution were Christians: nineteen Episcopalians, eight Congregationalists, seven Presbyterians, two Roman Catholics, two Quakers, one Methodist, and one Dutch Reformed Church member. A century and a half passed; dramatic growth and change occurred, but that commitment to Biblical Christianity endured.

The idea that America might become a secular country was not conceivable to those men. They did not even feel it was necessary to mention the word Christian in the Constitution, because that was the faith by which they were inspired, they felt assured it would continue to be respected by the government they framed. They were appalled and repelled by the anti-Christian excesses of the French Revolution. Because of their bad experiences with State Churches in England and on the Continent, they wisely began the Bill of Rights by affirming that religious freedom (including the right of religious people to express their views politically) was the most precious freedom of all.

Religious liberty has always been America's most cherished freedom. This was vividly illustrated when Parliament attempted to appoint bishops over the American churches. That unfortunate dictate helped to spark the American Revolution into flames.

The idea that the American political system, conceived in an environment that assumed Christianity to be the true faith, could later be turned around and used to restrict Christian liberty, was literally unthinkable to Americans in 1776.

Christians wrote the Constitution. They ran for public office, and served in the highest offices in the land. They established the schools, universities, and hospitals, and created a general climate of Christian influence throughout American history. In fact, it has only been in the last century that Bible believing Christians have retreated into piety, rather than practicing the Christian stewardship which makes us responsible for all of our blessings ... including this great nation "under God."

What has been the result of this apathy?

Tragic and unforgivable.

The Constitution, perverted by a willful Supreme Court (undeterred by an impotent Congress), has now become the tool used by humanists to secularize America. Flying in the face of historic precedents it is being used to erase all recognition of God from American public life.

The good news is that people of faith have now taken to the field, and that army is committed to returning America to the traditional values cherished by our Forefathers.

This helpful book about Christian activism is a manual to give guidance to concerned Christian Americans who wish to make their influence felt, and who are willing to stand up and make their voices heard.

To you, the Christian activist, this manual is dedicated with the hope that an aroused Christian citizenry can restore religious liberty to America, can preserve the life of the unborn, and can assure that our representatives in Washington will once more become aware of their responsibility to represent those values that have historically been our heritage.

INTRODUCTION

Christian influence upon America's national life has been a constant feature throughout our long history. From men of deep religious faith who, like John Witherspoon, gave birth to this nation "under God," through contemporary men and women who live out the Biblical implications of their faith, America has been richly blessed.

Unfortunately, many of us as Christians have ignored our responsibilities to be active and educated in our political process.

America suffers form moral decay, breakdown of the family unit, pornography, drug and alcohol abuse, violence, sexual perversion, and the threat to our religious liberty.

Today, people of faith are called to be involved in the political process. We are called to hold government accountable. We must hold our elected officials to standards of behavior and positions that are based on principle. It is our duty as citizens of this nation.

Let us, therefore, joyously accept personal responsibility for this good land. Let us identify the great ethical and moral questions that often find their way into legislation, and let us make our Christian voices heard.

The first step is in exercising our right to express our opinion at the ballot box. We encourage all people of faith to participate in the democratic process by voting, and by doing so as an informed voter.

But there are other ways to make our voices heard that require efforts beyond the voting booth. These methods are often referred to as "lobbying."

Although it has gained a negative connotation nowadays, lobbying is simply the practice of influencing governmental decisions and public policy. The term originated in the United States of the 1830s, when representatives of interest groups tended to congregate in the lobbies of Congress, state legislatures — and even the hotels where elected representatives stayed during their session.

And it doesn't take a high-priced attorney or public relations agent with Italian suits, expense accounts and a Washington, D.C., office to do it. You too can be a lobbyist.

This guide will deal with various aspects of basic lobbying techniques available to anyone, such as: how to write letters, make personal contact, launch petition campaigns, obtain press coverage, etc. It also offers tips on what things to do — and not to do — to make your lobbying most effective!

Some of the more intricate complexities of lobbying are intentionally not mentioned (such as House and Senate rules and other legislative procedures) in order to avoid confusion and to acquaint you with the basics of effective grassroots lobbying. Correctly putting these fundamental lobbying techniques into action should enable your voice and influence to make a greater impact in Washington, D.C.

And while the following recommendations relate to influencing legislators in Washington, many of these steps are also applicable in lobbying your own state and local elected officials.

ONE

THE DUTIES OF CHRISTIAN CITIZENSHIP

There may be those good Christians who have shied away from toiling in the political fields because of misguided convictions about mixing religion and government, or doubts about whether a true Christian should stoop to play the game of politics.

Yet how can we as Christian citizens expect God to restore righteous leadership, through us as his instruments, unless we are willing to get involved?

Fellow Christian leader and founder of the Campus Crusade for Christ ministry, the late Dr. Bill Bright, created the following outline of duties to help Christians practice both their faith and good citizenship:

Citizenship in a free country is a blessing from God. Our great system of self government assures every Christian a voice in the affairs of the nation. God wants us to do His will in government, just as in church and in the home.

But we have disobeyed our Lord. We have ceased to be the "salt of the earth" and the "light of the world," as Christ commanded. As a result, the moral fiber of America is rotting away – and our priceless freedom is in grave jeopardy. Atheism is penetrating every area of our national life. America is faced with the greatest crisis in its history. We are in danger of losing our nation by default, and with it our individual freedoms and possibly our very lives.

Some Christians refuse to accept responsibility as citizens because they feel politics is corrupt; they don't want to get soiled. But the political process is not inherently "dirty." It is in fact neutral. It is only when the political system is corrupted by immoral men (as a result of our sinful neglect) that it becomes "a dirty game."

The American political system offers Christians an unprecedented opportunity to serve His will, unheard of in most parts of the world. We sin before God if we fail to grasp that opportunity. Active participation in the political process by Christians is not an option. It is a mandate.

If this is to be a government "of the people, by the

people, and for the people," then, in order for it to function properly, every Christian citizen has a responsibility to register, to vote, to be informed and to actively influence others.

The great 18th century British statesmen and political thinker Edmund Burke said, "All that is necessary for the triumph of evil is for good men to do nothing." America is the last stronghold of freedom on earth – and citizens who are dedicated to God are the only resource for the preservation of our freedoms, including our freedom to serve Him. A few good men and women, following the simple guidelines contained in this book, can set this nation on a new course of righteousness for His glory.

Your Christian Citizenship Checklist

Being very honest with yourself, how would you answer the following questions:

- Do I pray faithfully for a spiritual revival to sweep America?

- Am I a registered voter?

- Do I encourage fellow Christians to register and vote?

- Am I making a serious effort, along with my

Christian friends, to become informed about issues that affect the morality of our nation?

- Am I actively involved in helping to select and elect good candidates for public office?

- Do I vote faithfully in every election for the best candidate, regardless of party?

- Do I stay involved in the process once I have left the voting booth?

If your answer to one or more of these questions was "no," this book is "must" reading for you. It will bring you to a new realization that faith in our Lord implies obligation and duty to serve Him in all areas of life – including citizenship. And what is far more important, it will show you how to practice your citizenship for His glory.

Your Five Duties as a Christian Citizen

1. Pray
2. Register to vote
3. Become informed
4. Help elect Godly people as public servants
5. Vote

Your First Duty: Prayer

We know from scripture that the rule of the wicked is a direct violation of the will of God. "For the wicked shall not rule the godly, lest the godly be forced to do wrong." (Psalm 125:3). God forbids the tyranny of the wicked. Instead, His plan calls for the rule of the righteous. God's promise to heal a repentant nation is also found in the Bible: "If My people will humble themselves and pray, and search for Me, and turn from their wicked ways, I will hear them from heaven and forgive their sins and heal their land." (II Chronicles 7:14)

So our first responsibility as Christian citizens is to pray that God will send a great spiritual awakening to America and that Christians will dedicate themselves to God for spiritual living and active service within the family, the church and the nation. Pray daily that the Spirit of God will enable you, by His power, to live a godly life and introduce others to Christ as their Savior – the first step to good citizenship.

Pray daily for God's guidance in how we can use our rights as an American citizen and our system of democratic government we have been endowed with by our Creator to be His instrument in directing the course of this nation. Pray so that righteous rule will be restored and our nation will turn from its sinful path to moral destruction.

And pray daily that men and women of God will be elected to public office at all levels of our government –

local, state and national – so that our land will be healed and our people can rejoice in righteous leadership, for "blessed is the nation whose God is the Lord…"

Along with earnest prayer…

Your Second Duty: Register to Vote

You must register as a qualified voter in order to practice your citizenship with accountability to God.

If you're not already registered, then you should do so at once by contacting your state board of elections office or other agencies that perform this service. In order to serve God as a citizen, you must become a regularly participating voter. But you cannot vote until you have taken the necessary steps for registration.

Why is it so important for you as a Christian to register? Because millions of God's people throughout America are not even registered to vote. How can we as Christian citizens expect God to restore righteous leadership through us, unless we are willing to take a few minutes to register? Only when you have registered to vote will you be in a position to help assure the election of godly officials. "Godliness exalts a nation…" (Proverbs 14: 34).

Voting is a matter of good stewardship under God. Register as soon as possible, so that you can vote in the next election, and every election, as a service for God. "The good influence of godly citizens causes a city to prosper..." (Proverbs 11: 11)

Once you have registered...

Your Third Duty: Become Informed

Organize and lead or participate in a study group to inform yourself and others concerning the structure of government, current problems and issues, and how to serve God effectively in the arena of politics at your own level of influence.

Just as the untrained soldier is at the mercy of his enemy, the uninformed Christian is incapable of prevailing against the forces of evil in the world of politics. In order to serve God effectively as a citizen of our country, you must know how to act for His glory within the framework of existing political systems and processes. Knowledge is essential to effective action. "...the wise man is crowned with knowledge." (Proverbs 14: 18) How can you best become an informed citizen?

Talk to your concerned Christian friends or fellow members of your congregation about starting a study group on responsible Christian citizenship. Outline for them your study group idea and show them samples of the materials you have located. With the group's agreement, set a date for your first meeting and plan to meet regularly thereafter.

Remember, delay can be fatal to the future morality of America. Don't allow anything to hinder your progress toward becoming a well-informed Christian citizen.

Christian Voice will help you in your research to become informed about issues affecting the moral character of our nation and the traditional values cherished by our Founding Fathers. Since our establishment in 1978, part of our ministry has been to encourage citizens to actively participate in the political process by providing information. You can contact us about a variety of our publications, by writing our headquarters at 208 North Patrick Street, Alexandria, Virginia, 22314 or calling (703) 548-1421. Or you may learn about the latest issues facing our leaders in Washington, D.C., by subscribing to our newsletter or visiting our web site, *www.christianvoiceonline.com*.

But knowledge is useless if it does not result in action...

Your Fourth Duty: Help Elect Godly People

The Book of Proverbs states a timeless principle: "When the righteous are in authority the people rejoice, but when the wicked beareth rule the people mourn." (Proverbs 29: 2) The question is, if God's people in America don't get involved politically, how will "the righteous" in America ever get into authority?

The most effective way to restore righteous rule and rejoicing in America is to elect godly people into positions of leadership. You must help select and elect men and women of God to public office at the local, state, and national levels, and support them faithfully throughout their terms of public service.

How can Christians accomplish this task? The word of God gives us the basic qualifications of a good candidate (Exodus 18: 16, 21-22), "I apply the laws of God. Find some capable, godly, honest men who hate bribes, and ... let these men be responsible to serve the people with justice at all times." The six qualifications included in this passage are: Godliness (spiritual maturity), Integrity, Industriousness, Biblical Guidance, Justice, and Demonstrated Capability (competence in managing business or professional affairs). Apply these God-given standards carefully and prayerfully in selecting your candidate.

Organizing in your local political precincts is the key to victory for a godly candidate. Secure the official precinct maps covering the district where your candidate is running for office. Become a precinct leader and encourage other Christians to take responsibility under God for their precincts as well. Enlist five to ten people to serve as a volunteer committee with each leader. Assign each volunteer to certain streets within the precinct so that all homes will be visited. There are only approximately 175,000 precincts in the entire United States, thus a relatively small handful of determined, godly people can wield great influence and help change the direction of this nation.

As a Christian precinct leader or volunteer, you will have a key role in the election of godly candidates. You can contribute by getting acquainted with the precinct's residents, enlisting additional volunteers, help your candidate's supporters register and, if necessary, personally assist in transporting them to the polls on election day.

A handful of dedicated Christians, each of whom will spend four or five hours every month in precinct service, can usually carry their precinct for a qualified candidate. If this can be done in a majority of the precincts in your election district, your candidate will win the election. Most important of all, your precinct service will give you an excellent opportunity to share God's love with your neighbors.

After the election is over, continue your precinct committee. Meet for prayer and fellowship at least monthly. Invite others to join you in your study group. With His guidance, plan ongoing precinct activities. Keep looking for and screening new candidates for various public offices at the local, state and national levels. Be aware of the best opportunities. Keep praying, keep serving, keep helping your neighbors, keep loving others and keep working for God.

And don't forget to exercise your privilege on election day...

Your Fifth Duty: Vote

Vote consistently in every election, after informing yourself concerning the various candidates and issues, and evaluating them on the basis of God's Word.

Only when you cast your ballot do you fulfill your Christian responsibility in government where voting is so strategically important. Exercise the citizen influence that God has given you through our unique system of self-government. If you fail to vote conscientiously for godly rule, evil will increase in our nation.

It is commonly said that decisions in America are made by a majority of the people. This is not so. Decisions are made by a majority of those who *participate*. As few as 16% of all eligible voters in a district can elect a member of Congress. Even presidents have been elected by an average of one-half vote per precinct nationwide.

How can you know for whom you should vote? Make a sincere effort to obtain reliable information about all issues and candidates before casting your ballot. In making your decision, you may read the candidate's literature, hear him speak, exam his platform, read news articles, talk with members of your congregation or pastor, study the Bible and ultimately, let the Word of God be your guide.

Remember that a candidate's principles are far more important than his party. Vote your Christian convictions in preference to your party. Through your Christian citizenship group, form a Candidate Selection Committee to evaluate the various candidates and report to the Christian public. To place confidence in unworthy candidates is a miscarriage of our Christian stewardship. "Putting confidence in an unreliable man is like chewing with a sore tooth, or trying to run on a broken foot." (Proverbs 25: 19)

Ongoing Stewardship after Election Day

In America, our legal system has its roots in God's

Law, the Ten Commandments and the Golden Rule. The Founding Fathers understood that our rights derived from God, not from any one man or body of men. Our early legislators tried to mold their legislation within scriptural guidelines as they interpreted them. Such a legal system, founded on universal truth, is therefore both constant and objective, and not subject to the temporary whims of man.

Laws based solely on the opinion and power of man or man-made institutions are constantly changing, are arbitrary in nature, and subject to abuse by those in control. Such a legal system is common to all non-democratic nations.

Unfortunately, we can see the same trend developing in America where the opinion of secular humanists – whether in the White House, Congress, the Supreme Court or the media – now reigns supreme, without any consideration of God's Law. We are losing sight of our bedrock principle that our nation follows the "rule of law and not of man." If this disturbing trend toward secular humanism accelerates, we shall lose more and more of the "inalienable rights" we have been endowed with by our Creator.

Under our Constitutional form of government, we are the government, through our elected representatives. If, by failing to accept and perform the Five Duties outlined above – and by not remaining involved after we cast our ballots – Christians allow their representatives (either by default or by active vote) to make laws that violate Christian conscience, then we as Christians are at least guilty before God of the grievous sin of omission, if not of commission.

Of this we can be very sure, Christian ethics and the clear directions of the New Testament place strong imperatives upon Christians in modern America. "He who knoweth to do right and doeth it not ... to Him it is sin."

We enjoy a government of the people, by the people, for the people. The decisions of our representatives are to be a reflection of the convictions of all the people. That includes America's huge Christian population. The failure of Christians to have their religious convictions reflected by their elected representatives in government is a spiritual failure. It is a failure of Christians to "let your light so shine before men that they will see your good works and glorify your Father which is in heaven." It is a failure of Christians to "Be like a city, set upon a hill whose light cannot be hid."

And lastly, here's what America's foremost Christian leader has to say on the subject of Christian involvement in the political process:

"On almost every front – political, economic, social, ecological – our world seems close to the breaking point... Secular humanism is still the dominant philosophy. Our national institutions – education for example – often exhibit a strong bias against Christian convictions.

"Instead of being a prophetic voice boldly declaring the clear Word of God to our secular society, we are instead tempted to become bland and innocuous, knowing that the world does not like prophets who challenge its cherished unbeliefs.

"Individual evangelicals should be active in the political arena, and I am thankful for those who have sensed a special calling to politics. Christians should get involved in good government – not to conform, but to transform."

—*Rev. Billy Graham*

Now that we've discussed the first duties of Christian citizenship, we'll examine in more detail how to continue making our influence felt in government – primarily Congress – as grassroots lobbyists in our ongoing capacity as good stewards of what God has blessed us with in the United States of America.

TWO

YOUR VOICE COUNTS, SO SPEAK UP

Perhaps the most common and damaging idea in America today is that one person's voice doesn't really count. It is understandable that people feel this way because your legislator will not always vote (sometimes never) according to your wishes.

However, it is extremely important to dispel the myth that your voice doesn't make a difference in how your legislator votes. Many times the expressed sentiment of constituents in a congressman's district is the decisive factor in how he or she may vote.

It is very important to remember that every elected official has one top priority — reelection. Consequently, legislators are sensitive to the opinions of their constituents. They realize that political survival can not be long assured if they consistently vote against or ignore the sentiments of the people "back home." Ultimately, it will be the cumulative impact of many voices, including your own, which will have the greatest impact on a legislator's vote. But if you do not contact your legislator, it will be one more voice lost to our side and, by default, give more influence to the voice of the other side on a legislator's vote.

One of the most important lessons to remember in lobbying is that your failure to act automatically increases the influence of the opposition. Legislators do not operate in a political vacuum. Especially when an important vote on an issue is to take place in Congress, legislators face enormous pressure from all sides.

It is an unfortunate fact of political life that the contest for influencing a legislator is often reduced to a war of numbers. For example, if a legislator receives 100 letters from pro-abortion forces in his district and only 10 letters from pro-life constituents, (if he is personally uncommitted on this issue) he is more likely to vote the pro-abortion position. Every letter counts! Don't ever be misled into believing your voice and opinion are not important.

Complacency and Disillusionment

The two seductive diversions from performing effective grassroots lobbying are complacency and disillusionment.

Complacency often develops in people after a pro-traditional, family values candidate is elected in their district. While this is undoubtedly good news, it cannot be taken for granted that this congressman will always or instinctively vote accordingly! Remember, this congressman may also be a "letter counter" and can often be pressured against his better judgment to vote according to the mail he receives.

Congressmen are also subject to a multitude of other pressures in Washington, D.C. (party leadership pressure for example), which can easily persuade them to vote contrary to your preferences — especially in the absence of any feedback from their constituents!

In addition, there are many who will make promises during the heat of a campaign to solicit conservative, Christian votes and then just as easily ignore those promises once elected. It is imperative to keep the pressure on congressmen to offset opposition influence and to make certain they fulfill their campaign promises.

Remember, never take a congressman's vote for granted. Even a "friendly" congressman needs to hear from you. Always avoid complacency.

Disillusionment is the other side of the coin that

can easily disaffect volunteers, especially newcomers to politics. Very often people will work very hard to influence a congressman's vote or pass some important legislation, and in the end lose on one or both counts. Having failed once or even twice, it is easy to "give up" and believe influencing your congressman is hopeless. That, of course, is the attitude of the defeatist.

The important thing is not how many battles we lose, but whether or not we win in the end. Should you give up in the beginning, then eventual defeat will become a self-fulfilling prophecy. Like the tortoise and the hare, the race is not always to the swift. Just as Thomas Jefferson correctly observed, "The price of liberty is eternal vigilance."

Mr. Jefferson's statement is one of the most profound expressions of what politics is all about. The forces of humanism, atheism and immorality never rest, nor should we. We are in this battle for the long haul. It is totally unrealistic to expect that we will win every legislative fight all the time. It is not uncommon to take many years and many defeats before a bill is successfully passed in Congress. In the end, those who have the perseverance, faith, and commitment will be the true victors and patriots.

THREE

FIRST, KNOW YOUR CONGRESSMAN

The first and most important step in lobbying is to become acquainted with your congressman. Important facts about him are necessary in order for you to proceed with the greatest effectiveness.

Of course, if you are not sure who your congressman is, you need to find out. And there are several easy ways to do this. You may call your local newspaper or contact a known political organization (local Republican or Democratic Party Committees). If you have access to the Internet, Christian Voice's web site is *www.christianvoiceonline.com*.

Here are some of the key questions you should know the answers to about your congressman:

1. What is your congressman's political affiliation — Republican, Democrat, or other?

2. When was he elected and by what margin?

3. Is he an entrenched incumbent or politically vulnerable?

4. Where does you congressman stand on the political spectrum — conservative, moderate, liberal, etc.?

5. Where does he stand on key moral issues? For example, is he pro-life, in favor of school prayer, opposed to same-sex unions, etc?

6. How did your congressman vote on key pro-faith and pro-family issues?

This last point is the most important. The real litmus test for a congressman's performance is how he votes. After all, this is why he was sent to Washington in the first place: to vote on behalf of the people he represents. If you are not sure how your congressman votes, then write Christian Voice for a copy of its Congressional Vote Index. This will provide you with a factual accounting of how your elected representative has voted on key moral issues.

Understanding your congressman's political affiliation, leanings, and voting record will greatly assist you in making the correct approach towards influencing their vote on a particular bill before Congress.

For example, if your congressman is a liberal and

has a pro-abortion stance, then you should take a strong, uncompromising approach on the issue, plus make certain he knows you are aware of his position/voting record. More than anything else, congressmen are deeply afraid that their constituents will know how they actually vote. Very often congressmen rely on the ignorance of their constituents to mislead them about their voting record. Many silk-tongued politicians have easily talked one way and voted another knowing their constituents will rarely know the difference. This knowledge of how your congressman votes gives you more power. Your command of the facts with him will give your own opinion greater weight and credibility and thus, your message will have more influence.

Should you discover that your congressman is basically in support of your position, then your letter should take an encouraging and more conciliatory tone. Praise him for his pro-life position, campaign promises, voting record, etc., but, make it clear you are watching closely how he will vote. Whether your congressman is friend or foe, it is always important he is aware that you are closely monitoring his performance.

Again, knowledge of how your congressman votes or stands on a key moral issue is critically important.

As Thomas Jefferson astutely observed: "If a nation expects to be ignorant and free, in a state of civilization, it expects what never was and never will be."

FOUR

MAKING CONTACT

The single most effective form of lobbying is through direct and indirect personal contact. Direct contact is through personal interaction with the congressman. The indirect approach usually involves dealing with a congressman's staff at the local or national level. Sometimes the latter is more important. For political/public relations reasons, a congressman will almost always appear to be affable and cooperative on a personal level. However, this is his political survival instinct, which may be more superficial than substantial.

Nonetheless, personal contact underscores many things: your personal concern, persuasiveness, knowledge, and the importance of the issue you are lobbying on behalf of. Congressmen are often insulated by their staff, which filters what they want the congressman to hear. The congressman may rarely, if ever, hear your point of view unless confronted directly. Equally important, however, is that you follow up with staff to make certain your message is having its fullest impact.

Direct Contact:
The Congressman on Your Turf

Most people can rarely afford the time and expense of visiting their congressman in Washington, D.C. Even if you cannot afford the trip to our nation's capital, there will be many occasions for you to meet and visit with your congressman in your own district. For obvious political reasons, a congressman will spend many weekends and holidays in his district to meet with constituents. Most often, a congressman will appear at an organized group function. Sometimes it will be a political event and many times, non-political, i.e., a groundbreaking ceremony, college commencement address, or charity fundraising affair. Whatever the occasion, this provides you with the best opportunity to confront your congressman face to face.

Discovering when and where your congressman will be in the area is extremely easy! Simply call his local district office to find out his itinerary. Plan to be at some event and bring as many friends as possible to reinforce your position. Don't worry if you cannot meet or talk with your congressman personally. Raising a point or asking a question from the audience is often more effective. After all, it's easier for a congressman to be evasive one-on-one than it is to "fool" a gathering of many people.

Congressmen rarely welcome being put on the spot before an audience, especially if the media are present, but there can be no more effective means of forcing them to make an "on-the-record" commitment for or against a political issue. While a congressman may try to give an evasive answer, the fact that he was forced to take a stand in front of the multitudes makes a significant impact on their political comprehension of what voters think "back home." And their voting behavior in Washington, D.C., will likely be more attuned accordingly.

Indirect Contact: The District Office Staff

Since opportunities to meet with your congressman will be few and far between, it is very important for you to establish a personal, on-going relationship with the key people in a congressman's district office. These district staff employees are the congressman's "eyes and ears" in the district and frequently report back on constituent concerns, what the local media is reporting about the congressman, where local organizations stand on issues, etc.

With few exceptions, most district staff have very little impact on legislative matters since much of their function involves individual casework of a non-political nature. However, they do serve as a barometer for the congressman on the political climate. Frequent visits, phone calls, and letters to district staff on a political issue will most certainly sound "alarm bells" in Washington.

And don't allow a district staffer to easily mollify your concerns or evade the responsibility to follow-up. Insist that they or the congressman provide you with an answer, position, and how he will vote on the issue you've raised.

Taking Your Message to Washington

If you're fortunate enough to be able to visit our nation's capital, then you can take your message right to Capitol Hill. But congressmen and senators are very busy people, so it is extremely important that you schedule an appointment as far in advance as possible.

Once inside the office door, due to their tight schedules, you will likely have only five-to-fifteen minutes to meet with your congressman. This makes it very important for you to get through the pleasantries and greetings as soon as possible, then move directly into the substance of the issue on which you are lobbying. People often make the mistake of wasting these precious minutes on "hometown" chit-chat and suddenly discover time has run out, the congressman's out the door and barely a word was uttered about the important issue they came to lobby about. Spend two or three minutes on greetings and introductions, but no more.

Whenever applicable, mention that you voted for the congressman and/or worked on his campaign. This automatically makes the congressman more indebted to you and more open to your message. Conversely, if you did not vote for your congressman, it is best not to mention it.

In addition, it is always more effective to identify yourself as a leader/member of an organized political group in the congressman's district. It is also helpful to mention what non-political clubs or church you support or hold membership in. Again, it is a matter of impressing upon a congressman that you speak on behalf of many other people who share your concerns. Congressmen are always much more impressed by numbers.

Before giving your congressman your lobbying message, it is helpful to first ask questions about where he stands on the particular issue. Once you know what the congressman's inclinations are on the issue, you can tailor your message more effectively. Try to find what chief concerns or problems, if any, he has on the issue. You might be able to provide him an answer to this dilemma or, at a minimum, get back to him with more information (studies, statistics, articles, etc.) that will assist in overcoming these concerns. After the meeting, make accurate notes of what the congressman said. This will be important for the necessary follow-up.

Congressmen may often be unavailable for meetings; therefore, you will have to talk to their legislative aide who handles the particular issue you wish to discuss. Always insist on talking with this legislative aide if the congressman is not available. Very often it is just as important to lobby these aides as it is the congressman. These aides have the greatest amount of influence on how a congressman votes. Should his aide remain unconvinced about your position on an issue, it usually follows that the congressman will likewise be opposed. Should the staff member be evasive or unable to give you an estimate of how the congressman will vote, insist that some kind of response (phone call or letter) be given to you at the earliest possible date.

A Thank You Note is More Than a Courtesy

After a meeting with a congressman or staff member, always follow up with a letter thanking them for the opportunity to meet with them and reiterating your position on the issue. Aside from being a simple courtesy, these letters remind the congressman and/or staff member about your position on an issue and reinforces the importance of your views. It's one more shot at getting your message across.

In fact, letters are so vital to grassroots lobbying, the entire next chapter is devoted to writing them and how to organize a letter writing campaign.

FIVE

LETTERS: AN EFFECTIVE TOOL

Letters are the easiest and the most often employed medium of expressing views to our elected representatives in Washington, D.C. While sending a letter may not seem to be the most effective tool in persuading a congressman, they are extremely important in making your voice heard.

Letters serve as a means for a congressman to judge the depth and breadth of the sentiment "back home" on a particular issue. And they do this in two ways — volume and contents.

Total numbers are the most important to a congressman. Rarely will a congressman actually read his constituent mail. This time-consuming task falls to his staff. Periodically, a staff member will compute the number of letters on an issue and provide the congressman with the total pro and con figures. The advantage, of course, is to the side with the greatest number of letters. As Marshall McLuhan said, the medium is the message.

In addition to the quantity factor, letters should also have a qualitative value. This is reflected in its contents. The more well written, thoughtful and accurate a letter is, the greater its impact will be. Don't dilute the importance of your message by using poor grammar, erroneous statements and sloppy, barely legible handwriting. (But better a sloppy letter, however, than none at all!)

Since you are representing a Christian viewpoint and are concerned about biblical principles, your letter should likewise reflect the quality of the important message you are trying communicate through your use of language and tone.

Sample Contents of a Letter

Always keep you letters brief and to the point. Try not to exceed one page. It's not the quantity of the words, but rather the quality of the message that counts.

The following is a brief outline of the contents your letter should include (a sample can be found at the end of this chapter):

First Paragraph: State the bill, amendment, or issue about which you are concerned and your basic position (for or against). Include the bill number whenever possible.

Second Paragraph: Elaborate on the reasons for your position. Include facts, statistics, cost figures, Biblical references, potential consequences, and anything else you think will add to the credibility and persuasiveness of your position.

Third Paragraph: Ask your congressman to indicate his position and how he intends to vote on the issue. Indicate you are expecting a reply and that you intend to share it with friends, relatives, members of your church, local media and/or political organizations of which you are a member. Also ask him to let you know how he did vote on the issue.

A Dozen Dos and Don'ts of Letter Writing

1. Whenever possible, do use the stationery of an organization, corporation, or church. This indicates that you represent many more people than just yourself. Remember, numbers count!

2. Do indicate your address and date on both the letter and envelope. "Mystery" authors rarely are read and never receive a reply.

3. Senators and Representatives are formally addressed as the Honorable. The salutation, however, should read "Dear Senator/Representative Jones."

4. Don't make your letter more than one typewritten page. Make certain your letters are legible, brief, and to the point.

5. Do make sure your facts and statistics are correct. Include documentation and sources ... "According to Professor John Doe..."

6. Do enclose additional information that supports your arguments, such as newspaper clippings, magazine or newsletter articles, studies or reports, and fact sheets.

7. Whenever applicable, mention that you voted for the congressman, did volunteer work on his behalf during the election, and contributed to his campaign.

8. Don't use form letters and stilted institutional language. In your own words, explain why this issue is important to your community, children, school, business, etc. Make it as personable as possible.

9. Don't use threatening language. Be passionate but reasonable. Avoid giving a "fruitcake" image. Don't be hostile, abusive, or disrespectful in any way! You can be polite and still be firm.

10. Do write the congressman's legislative assistant, especially if you have talked with him before. You are likely to get better results.

11. Insist on receiving a reply answering how the congressman intends to vote on the issue. Most congressional replies are vague and avoid making firm commitments. Don't be satisfied with this response. Write your congressman again and let him know you consider his "evasive" reply totally inadequate. Don't let him off the hook. Keep the pressure on him to give you a straightforward and honest reply.

12. After the vote occurs, write your congressman and thank him if he voted correctly. Congressmen do not receive enough praise when they do the right thing. Also, the opposition will certainly write him to protest. He needs to have positive feedback just as much as input prior to the vote. Conversely, should he vote the wrong way, make sure you complain.

How Often Should You Write?

Finally, the frequency of how often you write is very important. You can write too often or too little. Once a month is more than sufficient. You don't want to give the impression you are just a "sunshine patriot or summer soldier" who isn't dedicated to the cause. Nor do you want to appear as some "crank" whose only interest is in continuously "harassing" a congressman. Often the once- or twice-a-week letter writer is the butt of jokes in a congressional office and is rarely taken seriously.

So the best advice is to only write when there is some extremely important issue before Congress you are deeply concerned about. Limiting your letters to these occasions will enhance your letter's' credibility and sincerity.

Organizing Letter Writing Campaigns

Remember, most congressmen are letter counters! In addition to getting your message sent to a congressman, it is extremely important for hundreds and thousands of other people to do the same. Don't forget that the opposition to your viewpoint is also actively flooding your congressman with communications. Therefore, it is critically important to maximize the numbers! The next chapter discusses how.

SAMPLE LETTER TO A CONGRESSMAN

First Independent Church of God
1776 Main St., Liberty, South Carolina, 29001

April 19, 2002
Hon. Jefferson Smith
United States House of Representatives
Washington, DC 20515

Dear Representative Smith,

I am writing to express my concern about
H.R. 217 now before Congress. I am opposed to
the passage of this bill regarding "Gay
Rights."Granting special rights to homosexuals
that other Americans don't have is not only
unfair, it is a betrayal of the Judeo-Christian
values this nation was founded on. In addition,
I fear such "rights" will force schools, sports
teams, day care centers, summer camps, churches
and other groups to hire gays and lesbians,
making our children easy prey for homosexual
predators. As a constituent who has voted for
you, I urge you to stand firm against H.R. 217.

I would appreciate hearing from you about
how you will vote on H.R. 217. I'm confident I
will be able to tell my friends, neighbors and
my church that you have listened and taken positive action to defend America's morality.

Thank you for your efforts and may God
continue to guide you and bless you.

Sincerely,

Jane Doe

SIX

HOW TO MULTIPLY ONE INTO MANY

There are several methods for generating increased constituent participation to influence a congressman. Briefly outlined, these methods include group/church captains, telephone banks, petitions, telegrams, mailgrams, and postcards. Without spending much time or effort, you can maximize communications to a congressman a hundred-fold by implementing one or a combination of these procedures.

Enlist as a Group/Church Captain

In the political lexicon, "captain" is a label for a person who takes on the responsibility to politically educate and activate a specific group or territory of people. Most often the term applies to people who, during elections, work to turn out voters for their Party's candidate, i.e., precinct or block captains.

Without even realizing it, most people have easy access to reach others who are sympathetic to their point of view — people who will likely write their congressmen. Providing them the information and motivation to write letters requires very little time, expense, or effort.

Plan to become the captain of the organization or church to which you belong. Make it your responsibility to provide members of this group/church with information about key legislation and urge them to write their congressmen or senators.

The easiest method of educating your colleagues and fellow parishioners about important legislation is to make photocopies of a Legislative Alert and hand them out at the regularly scheduled group meeting or church service. The contents of a Legislative Alert should be patterned after your own letter to the congressman. If you do not have time to prepare a Legislative Alert, then simply reproduce your own letter to the congressman and distribute copies. In addition, you may wish to pass out copies of an article on the issue you've clipped from a newspaper, magazine, or newsletter.

Obtain your pastor's permission to distribute these Legislative Alerts during the Sunday School adult

Bible study classes, and post them on the church bulletin board. Should your pastor share your concern on the issue, urge him to make an announcement during Sunday service about the issue and for people to contact you if they need more information.

Cultivate Your Telephone Tree

Very often a key vote on an issue may occur in Congress with only a few days notice. This will not allow you the time to notify people to write their congressmen by utilizing the Legislative Alert process. Nor will there be sufficient time to send communications through the mail to your congressman.

Therefore, the only way to reach other people and influence your congressman is by use of the telephone. It is extremely important for you to contact as many people as possible during this process.

There are two methods for setting up a telephone bank operation:

The first, and easiest, method is to make a roster of the names and telephone numbers of people who belong to your group or church. Most churches already have such a list of all its members that you can obtain from your pastor. Some even publish a membership directory. Call at least 10 of these people (more if you can) and urge them to also alert others — friends, neighbors, relatives, etc.

If you can, contact leaders or members of groups (political and non-political), they can make phone calls to their members as well. Enlist the support of anyone you consider sympathetic. For example, a friendly businessman can urge his employees or members of his Rotary club to also make calls to the congressmen. Christian school principals are another excellent source of support. Also, make certain local Christian radio and TV stations are notified, and urge them to alert their audiences.

The second and equally effective method is to establish a "phone tree" operation. This entails recruiting at least 10 other volunteers who will be willing to contact another 10 people to make calls to the congressman. Using this method, you only have to make 10 calls to reach 100 people. These 100 contacts should also be encouraged to alert others. There's no limit to the growth of your phone tree!

Recruiting phone tree volunteers is not very difficult. The ideal volunteer should be an active leader/member of another group or church. They in turn can develop their own phone tree operation within that organization or church. Similar to the first method, you can establish a phone tree operation within your own church. For example, if your church has 100 adult members enlist 10 volunteers who will divide up the remaining 90 members (nine each) for follow-up phone contact. Make certain each volunteer keeps a roster of these persons' names, including home and work telephone numbers.

If your church does not already have a telephone committee, you will need to form one using as many volunteers as you can get. (If one exists, however, you may wish to enlist more help at this time).

It is best if you choose a Telephone Committee Chairman to handle the details pertaining to the Telephone Committee. As the chairman, he or she will:

- Secure the most up-to-date list of all members of your congregation, and divide it into lists of 20 names each.

- Recruit sufficient numbers of callers for the phone bank (if this has not already been done) so that each caller is responsible for no more than 20 names.

- Give each of the callers the following: a calling list; the Legislative Alert on the issue; and an outline or even a "script" of what to say when they make the call.

- Contact each caller the day before the designated date the calls are to begin, reminding them of their task and asking if they have any last-minute questions or problems.

You and each caller should have the following information:

1. A list of names and phone numbers of the members of your congregation totaling 20 people.

2. A Legislative Alert or other background on the issue

3. An outline or "script" of what you are to say.

You should make sure the phone numbers on your list are accurate and up-to-date. Once having double-checked the list, it is your duty to make the calls and see that your people contact their congressman.

The Telephone Committee Chairman will brief you on the proper procedure, however, a general explanation follows below:

The first call should be made as soon as your chairman makes you aware of the issue, to give your writers enough time to produce and mail their letters. The purpose of this first call is three fold:

To remind the letter writer that an important piece

of legislation is coming up for a vote, and to urge them to make sure to contact their congressman about it.

Remind them to use the Legislative Alert you passed out at church for the basis of their letter or phone call. If they have misplaced it, then give them a brief rundown of the issue, the congressman's record and the Christian position.

Find out if anyone else in the household could also write a letter, such as an older parent or child of voting age, and urge them to join the effort.

The second call should be made closer to the vote on the legislation and the caller should inquire if the writer has sent a letter. If they have, thank them and cross their name from the list. If they have not, then the caller should remind them again how important it is that they perform their duty as Christians. Remind them that the issue will be decided soon, so their help is urgently needed.

After that, calls should be made, as needed for those who have not yet written, every week or few days until the vote is over.

Such a program carried out through the churches can be extremely effective in achieving our moral goals through legislation, and turning our nation back towards His will.

With the efforts of your church, and thousands of other churches across our land, results can be a monumental testament to God's power, and His glory.

Calling Your Congressman

Unless you know your congressman personally, it is unlikely you will be able to speak to him on the phone. Therefore, it is extremely important that you talk to the right person in his office who handles the legislative issue you wish to discuss. Get his name. Then don't waste your time talking to the receptionist who answers the phone. Insist on talking to the legislative aide who is responsible for advising the congressman on the issue.

When talking to the legislative aide, keep your conversation short and similar to the contents of a letter. Identify yourself as a registered voter in the congressman's district. Whenever applicable, also add that you voted for him, made a contribution and/or worked as a volunteer during his election campaign. If you can also identify yourself as the head of a particular group, or pastor of a church, then all the better.

Avoid being argumentative. If you have important facts and you really know the subject matter, then feel free to impress these salient points on the aide; jot a few notes or an outline before calling if it helps. Of course, the most important thing is that you called! Simply let the aide know where you stand and urge the congressman to vote "yes" or "no" on the particular issue.

Just like letters, at the end of the day, it will be the total number of calls made which will most impress a congressman.

Some people may be reluctant to make long distance calls because of the expense. This is not necessary. Simply call the administrative aide in the congressman's local district office. These district aides communicate daily with the congressman's office in Washington, D.C., and will pass along your message.

If you do not know you congressman's telephone number in Washington, then call the Capitol Switchboard number, (202) 224-3121, and they will connect you to the congressman's office.

Petitions

Petitions also offer an easy method of involving large numbers of people to lobby a viewpoint with a congressman. They also can provide you with a list of potential volunteers, members, or contributors to your own organization.

Since petitions are not as effective as letters or phone calls, it is important to have a large number of signatures. With petitions, quantity always counts! Follow these easy steps to draft and use a petition:

1. Clearly indicate to whom your petition is being sent — your congressman, the President, etc.

2. Keep the statement short and to the point — not more than one paragraph. The longer the petition's statement, the less likely people will bother to read it and, of course, add their signatures.

3. Allow sufficient space for people to sign their names. Not more than 15 signatures per page.

4. Make certain you include columns for a person's name, address, city, state, and zip code.

5. Be sure to tell people (or indicate on the petitions) where it should be returned. There should only be one collection point from which they will be sent en masse to the congressman. It is far more impressive to have 100 petitions sent to you congressman than to have them "trickle in" one at a time, scattered over a period of several weeks.

6. Set a specific deadline as to when all petitions must be returned.

7. Allow space at the bottom of the petition for name,

address and telephone number of the person circulating the petition.

8. Be sure to make photocopies of the petitions before forwarding them on to the appropriate party. These names will be invaluable later on for future political activity.

Postcards

There are two types of postcards, personal and impersonal. Both provide a fast and inexpensive way of communicating with your congressman. And they let you take advantage of the cheaper postal rate for mailing a postcard (no larger than 4 x 6 inches). However, neither have the impact of a written letter.

The personal postcard message can be handwritten or typed on any postcard purchased in a store. Pick one with a colorful picture or cartoon that will attract attention in a congressman's mail. Obviously, you will have to keep the message short but make certain you include how you want the congressman to vote, '"yes" or "no," on what specific issue.

You can also have a "postcard party." Purchase a large quantity of post cards, invite people to your home and serve refreshments. Everyone can then write their own message, or copy messages onto many postcards for distribution to others for them to sign. You can also arrange for this activity to be a part of your next regularly scheduled group or church function.

Impersonal postcards have a preprinted message on one side with the congressman's name and address on the other. Many such postcards can be produced very inexpensively at a quick-print shop. Distribute these postcards to members of your organization or church for them to sign and mail.

Always make certain people include their name and address on the postcard.

Telegrams and Mailgrams

Telegrams and mailgrams do pack a "punch." They are a dramatic, fast and effective means of getting your message noticed. When time is of the essence, they are the quickest method of communicating a message to your congressman, except for a phone call or fax.

Mailgrams are more often sent since they are much less expensive than a telegram. Make the message brief and similar in format to the contents of a letter. The minimum charge is usually for about 50 words.

Remember, even a simple message has significant impact because it is a mailgram.

When it becomes clear an urgent mailgram message is necessary, follow these easy steps:

1. First write your message and keep it to less than 100 words.

2. Call the Western Union office and read them the message. The charge will be included in your next telephone bill.

3. Alert others to do the same by utilizing the steps in the phone bank operation.

4. You can also leave your message with a Western Union operator for others to send. All people have to do is call this operator, give their name and phone number and indicate they want your message sent under their own name.

Mailgrams have two other advantages: one, they usually cost less than long distance telephone calls when an urgent message is required; and two, they are an attractive alternative for people who feel ill-equipped to discuss the issue over the phone with a congressman's aide.

Letters-To-The-Editor

Letters-to-the-editor are another effective means of influencing your congressman. Simultaneously, they can accomplish three things: one, educate the public about an important legislative issue; two, alert others to also write their congressman; and three, indirectly influence a congressman's vote on the issue.

Don't be discouraged if your letters are not always printed. The important thing is that some letters will be printed and your message communicated. The chances of your letter being printed will be enhanced if you observe the following tips:

- Make the letter topical, related to newsworthy events currently reported in the newspaper.

- The letter could be in reference to an editorial, column, or news story that has appeared in the newspaper or another letter-to-the-editor. State whether you agreed or disagreed with the opinions or slant of these articles.

- Write about things that would have an obvious impact on your community.

- Offer your opinions about important national problems and your solution to those problems.

- Try to get others to also write letters on the same subject. Like congressmen, newspaper editors are impressed with numbers. The more letters sent on a particular issue, the more likely at least one or all will get printed.

Dos and Don'ts for Letters-To-The-Editor

Do address your envelope and salutation to "Letter-to-the-Editor." Don't address it to the name of the newspaper's editor. Such a letter may be misconstrued as a personal missive and, thus, not get printed.

Do keep the letter brief. The longer it is, the more likely it will be edited and the less likely it will be printed due to space limitations.

Do stick to the facts or points you wish to make. Some wit or humor is helpful, but not necessary.

Do mention your congressman's name in the letter. This virtually guarantees the letter will be clipped and brought to his attention.

Don't be wrathful, self-righteous, or judgmental. The letter should have a courteous tone.

Do state at the beginning the author, date, and title of a column or editorial you are responding to in your letter. For example: "John Doe's column of January 21

'A Defense of Partial Birth Abortion' was totally off the mark ..."

Do use the stationery of an organization of which you are a member, which not only adds to your credibility but may catch the editor's eye — and even suggest a story.

Do include your home and work addresses and telephone numbers. Many newspapers require this information for verification before publication.

Press Releases

Using the media is very important. The more you can publicize an issue or the activities of your organization, the more influence you will have on a congressman. Again, congressmen are sensitive to, and impressed by, local media coverage.

Press exposure also enhances the credibility and influence of your organization. It's important that your congressman, and the media, be aware of your organization's existence and activities. Always notify the media of your group's events, rallies, speakers, or positions on key legislation.

You will find a sample news release at the end of this section.

How to Write a News Release

Below are the basic steps to writing a news release:

1. Use your organization's stationery or have special news release stationery printed. Make certain it is on photocopy-quality paper for future reproduction.

2. Include the appropriate heading, date, name, and phone number of the person to be contacted at the beginning.

3. The first paragraph, or lead, should include the five W's – who, what, when, where, why? Put the basic, salient information up front. The remainder of the release will provide further details and explanations.

4. The second paragraph should quote you or the group's chief spokesman stating something of importance. Try to use short, catchy, quotable phrases. If the language is dull and drawn out, you have less chance of being quoted.

5. The last paragraph should include more information about your group, i.e., when was it founded, how many members, what is its basic purpose, etc.

6. End each release by typing -30- or ### center spaced, below the last paragraph to indicate the end.

Give Your News Release a Professional Polish

By employing the following suggestions, you can give your news release the professional touch that will help it get noticed among the blizzard of paper landing on an editor's desk every day. Remember, the easier you make it for the busy newspaper editor to use your release, the more likely it will appear in print.

- It is very important for your press release to have a "handle" or "angle," i.e., what is the most important, newsworthy aspect of your press announcement. For example, "Christian Group Announces Plan to Register 10,000 Voters," or "Christian Group Launches Campaign to Defeat Gay Rights Ordinance." Try to highlight the significance of your activities and add drama.

- Don't waste words. Use short sentences and paragraphs.

- Press releases must always be typewritten.

- Double space between lines. If it's hard for an editor to read or edit, then it will not be reported or printed.

- Always make sure your facts, statistics, etc. are accurate. Double check!

- Make certain the release is proofread and checked for errors and grammatical mistakes.

- Deliver your release to the press at least one day prior to the date of the release. If it arrives late, the release will be considered "old news" and thrown away.

- Whenever possible, address the release to the reporter who covers the issues, or "beat," your press announcement is concerned with. If you are not certain which appropriate reporter to send the release to, then address it to the "News Editor."

- Make sure your release is sent to the local Associated Press and United Press International wire services. They both print a daily log announcing important group events, press conferences, etc. Also, if they cover your story, it automatically goes to every major news outlet in your locality/state.

- Follow up with phone calls to make certain the reporter or news editor did see your release. Sometimes a release may get misplaced or buried at the bottom of the mail and not seen for days.

SAMPLE NEWS RELEASE

Tulsa Christian Alliance
123 Any Street   For Immediate Release
Tulsa, OK 12354   April 21, 2002
                               Contact: Bill Jackson
NEWS RELEASE   (555) 555-5656
Tulsa Christian Alliance to
Register 10,000 Voters

The Tulsa Christian Alliance announced today that it will launch a massive voter registration drive to turn out 10,000 new evangelical, Christian voters in the next election. Over 100 area churches have already signed up to assist in the group's ambitious campaign.

Tom Jones, chairman of the organization, stated: "Christians have a civic duty and moral responsibility to be active in the political affairs of their nation. Too many Christians are not registered to vote. Our goal is to register at least 10,000 new voters by October 1."

The Tulsa Christian Alliance is establishing voter registration workshops at local churches and over 35 volunteer voter registrars will set up outside of churches on Sunday mornings between August 3 and September 30.

Founded in January 1980, The Christian Action Alliance of Tulsa is a non-profit group whose goal is to organize and educate area Christians into effective political action. Among other issues, the group favors pro-life legislation and the return of voluntary prayer in public schools. The group has over 1,000 members including 57 pastors.

###

SEVEN

WHO MAKES THE BEST LOBBYIST?

The person who potentially is the best lobbyist is one who is a very close friend, advisor, or contributor of your congressman. Like everyone else, a congressman usually has a small circle of his closest friends. These people could be almost anyone – old high school chums, wealthy financial supporters, a minister, reporter, relative, etc.

These people are the ones in whom a congressman confides, trusts, and respects. Their political judgment and advice is highly valued by a congressman. Equally important, these people have access. They can reach a congressman directly when all others might fail. It is very important to find out who these people are. Often local reporters or political party activists will have this information.

These people are much more accessible to you than a congressman, and can sometimes become

allies. Contact one or more of them when an important vote on an issue is before Congress. Persuade
them about the importance of the issue and urge them
to contact the congressman, and lobby on behalf of
your position. Very often it is that one phone call
from a friend the congressman highly respects and
trusts that can make a difference.

In politics, it is often not what you know, but who
you know that counts. These trusted friends of a congressman are in the best position to influence his
opinion and how he votes. Don't be bashful about
approaching these people. You may be surprised.
These people are often grateful to you for bringing the
vote or issue to their attention.

Other people who are also important are the officials of the local Party apparatus. For example, if your
congressman is a Republican, contact the local G.O.P.
county chairman. You can bet this person is well con-
nected with the congressman. After all, the congressman relies heavily on the funds and volunteers of the
local Party committees to win re-election.

State and local elected officials also carry great
weight with a congressman, especially if they are
members of the same political Party. Contact your
state legislator, county commissioner, school board

chairman or city councilman and urge them to exercise whatever influence they have on the congressman. They probably know the congressman personally, and their support and endorsements are especially important during re-election campaigns. Elected officials usually make the best lobbyists to their colleagues — don't be afraid to ask for their help.

EIGHT

A WORD ABOUT LOBBYING
AND THE LAW

There's one last thing to be aware of before you
embark on your new roll as a grassroots lobbyist
— the legal restraints on legislative activities for religious organizations.

A church may not engage in any kind of "substantial" legislative activities. Substantial is generally
defined as being a percentage of the church's expen-
ditures; and that expenditure is usually considered to
be anything above 5% of the church's total annual
budget.

Pastors and laymen may involve themselves in legislative activities, as individuals, without endangering
the tax-exempt status of the church.

The key is whether you are lobbying as a church,
i.e., sending out letters, etc., which state that the First

Independent Church takes a "no" stand on abortion, or whether your membership sends letters, etc., on their own as individuals.

A church may give its mailing list to a legislative effort on the same basis that it gives it to other organizations. However, if any special considerations are given to the legislative effort concerning the list, the cost of those considerations must be considered an expenditure, and included within the 5% a church is generally allowed.

The best advice is to always have your church check with its attorney or accountant if your congregation plans on launching a major grassroots lobbying effort. The actual precentage of what is defined as "substantial" legislative activity really depends on the church's expenses, receipts and how they are reported on its tax records.

ABOUT CHRISTIAN VOICE

Christian Voice was established in 1978 as a national political lobby and educational organization that represents traditional American values in Congress and across the country. It was the first of the "Christian Right" groups, predating the Christian Coalition, Coalition for Traditional Values, Concerned Women for America, and many other groups. CV has always welcomed the opportunity to share its knowledge and expertise with groups that were formed after it. Today, Christian Voice is pleased to see so many pro-family organizations emulating it and following in its path.

Christian Voice is best known as the originator and developer of the "Congressional Report Card" and the "Candidates Scorecard." Christian Voice pioneered grassroots action through use of the "Church Networking Guide."

During the past quarter century, our other activities have included:

- Defending Christian schools against government harassment

- Leading the Prayer in School fight through our Washington, D.C., lobby and our National Prayer Coalition of 100 national organizations.

- Providing a moral issues voting record on every member of Congress to millions of Christians, including key leaders, pastors, and national organizations.

- Opposing Gay Rights laws in Congress. (Christian Voice is credited by the national gay rights lobby as being their major obstacle.)

- Reaching 60 million Americans through the mass media. (Christian Voice was voted the top story of the year by the religious writers and editors of America.)

- Publicizing the voting record of congressmen on key issues in over 1,500 newspapers.

- Maintaining a large force of Christian and conservative lobbyists in Washington.

- Regularly supplying crucial information to 40,000 ministers and thousands of Christian radio and TV stations to inform their audiences on critical moral issues before Congress.

- Working on behalf of Pro-Life spokesman Dr. C. Everett Koop's Senate confirmation as Surgeon General in the Reagan Administration.

- Broadcasting hard-hitting media specials from 60-minute prime time features to 60-second TV and radio commercials on thousands of stations, featuring major movie stars and Christian leaders telling millions of Christians how and when to write their congressman on key issues when they come before Congress.

Our successful role in many legislative battles has made us the subject of more than 7,000 feature articles in publications such as *Newsweek, Time,* and *U.S. News & World Report* and on TV programs such as *60 Minutes, ABC News Special Report, 20/20,* and *Good Morning America.*

What the Media says about Christian Voice

60 Minutes – "Millions of Christians appear to be coming together to form a new powerful force. In the vanguard is Christian Voice...CV is being heard in Washington, DC, loud and clear!"

Dan Rather, CBS News – "Among the largest and most influential of the groups trying to ... re-establish the nation's Christian foundation is Christian Voice."

Newsweek Magazine – "The prospect of such a powerful political force [Christian Voice] worries liberals..."

U.S. News & World Report – "Conservative ministers and lobbyists are out to arouse the sleeping giant of American politics... millions of evangelical Christians who say they have enough votes to change the course of U.S. history ... In the vanguard of the drive is a fast-growing political-action group called the Christian Voice."

Los Angeles Times – "The lobby, known as Christian Voice, is sponsoring a $350,000 plus ad campaign to push its causes."

The Washington Post – "Christian Voice ... has already initiated mass mailing campaigns, produced television ads and begun raising money to fund a number of lobbying efforts. Goals include tax breaks for church run schools and the frustration of the abortion and gay rights movements."

Des Moines Register – "Probably the most notorious of the several groups in the movement is the Christian Voice, because of its widely publicized 'morality rating' of the voting records of the members of Congress."

Miami Herald – "In the Presidential race, the

Christian Right, particularly Christian Voice, may have had its biggest impact..."

Christian Voice's Leadership

Dr. Robert Grant is the founding chairman of Christian Voice, the nation's oldest conservative Christian lobby. In addition to helping start the California Graduate School of Theology, Dr. Grant is one of the founders of the United Community Church of Glendale, California. He has served in ministerial positions in Baptist and independent churches.

After graduating from Wheaton College in Wheaton, Illinois, with a Bachelor of Arts in History, Dr. Grant went on to earn a Bachelor of Divinity and a Master of Divinity from Fuller Theological Seminary in Pasadena, California; and a Doctor of Philosophy from the California Graduate School of Theology. He was also awarded a diploma from the St. Paul Bible College in St. Paul, Minnesota.

Dr. Grant has authored numerous articles and books on religious and patriotic themes. In recognition of his many trips to the Holy Land – some 125 during a 20-year period – he was awarded the Shalom Award by the Government of Israel. He is also a member of the Publisher's Council of the *Conservative Digest*.

In his capacity as a leader in the traditional values movement, Dr. Grant has appeared on *60 Minutes*, CBS and NBC news, the *Morton Downey Jr. Show*, *Good Morning America*, CBS *Nightwatch* and numerous local and national radio and television talk shows. His activities have been reported in *Time*, *Newsweek*, *U.S. News & World Report*, the *Washington Post*, *Christianity Today*, and hundreds of other publications across America.

Born in 1936, Dr. Grant is married to Judy Joanne Grant.

Gary L. Jarmin has been a key leader, strategist and lobbyist in the conservative and evangelical movements for more than 30 years. He has served as the legislative director for the American Conservative Union, director of the American Coalition for Traditional Values voter registration drive and is currently president of The Seniors Center, a ministry of Christian Voice.

Mr. Jarmin pioneered the development in religious organizations of grassroots political organizing techniques still used today. He is the author of the "Congressional Report Card on Key Moral/Family Issues" published by Christian Voice, as well as the developer of the organization's Candidate Index. His voter registration efforts added an estimated 2 million new names to the voter rolls. He has been involved in many election and lobbying campaigns.

In addition to domestic issues, Mr. Jarmin has been very active in mobilizing conservative foreign policy. He has organized and escorted dozens of delegations of prominent American political leaders to visit countries in Asia and has met with numerous heads of state.

A well-respected political commentator, Mr. Jarmin has made numerous appearances on radio and television, including CNN, *Good Morning America*, *20/20*, ABC, CBS and NBC news, and has been quoted by hundreds of major news publications.

A native Californian, Gary and his wife Gina live in Virginia. They have three sons.

How to Contact Us

For more information on any of the topics discussed in this book, or to learn more about our ministry contact:

Christian Voice
208 North Patrick Street
Alexandria, VA 22314
(703) 548-1421
or visit us at www.christianvoiceonline.com

Other Christian Voice Publications

Christian Voice produces a number of publications that are useful tools for people of faith to become more involved in the public policy process:

The Christian Voice Guides to....

Your Five Duties as a Christian

Questions and Answers Relating to Homosexuality

Abstinence Education and Sex-Education Reform

Church Networking Guide

The next handbook in Christian Voice's
series for reclaiming America!

Saving the Shining City
Rebuilding America One Vote at a Time

In its first book, "Building the Shining City,"
Christian Voice condensed 25 years of experience as
the pioneer of modern religious activism into an easy-
to-follow grassroots-lobbying guide for Christian citizens who want to make an impact on our leaders in
Washington.

Now, in "Saving the Shining City" you'll learn how
you can have the same influence on the ballot box.
Within its pages, Christian Voice answers any concerns about why Christians should get involved in
politics and shows you how good people can rescue
America's government. Discover the four basic steps
of increasing Christian participation in the election
process and other grassroots techniques for electing
Godly men and women to serve in public office.

Coming in Spring 2004
Look for it at **www.christianvoiceonline.com**

How You Can Help Build an America based on Faith and Family Values

This book can have a powerful impact on our country's morality and its future — if you and others act now. Please give copies to your family, friends and neighbors so all good Christians can learn the basic lobbying techniques that will help them stand up for traditional family values.

By distributing as many copies as you can, you will be supporting one of Christian Voice's most important grassroots educational campaigns, and you could be deciding the outcome of pro-faith, pro-family issues – as well as the fate of America.

Building the Shining City Order Form

Single Copy $4.95   Two Copies $8.00   Three Copies $11.00

(Please add a $2 shipping and handling fee to your total.)

Please send me _____ copies of the book, "Building the Shining City: The Grassroots Lobbying Guide for Christian Activists." Enclosed is my check for $_____ payable to Christian Voice.

Name:_____

Address:_____

City:_____ State:____ ZIP:_____

Christian Voice
P.O. Box 966
Frederick, MD 21705

Learn more about our ministry by visiting our web site at
www.christianvoiceonline.com

Christian Voice is a 501(c)(4) non-profit organization, gifts to which are not deductible as charitable contributions for Federal income tax purposes. A copy of the latest financial report and registration filed by this organization may be obtained by contacting us at: 208 North Patrick St., Alexandria, VA 22314 703-548-1421 or by contacting any of the state agencies: *California: Christian Voice's audited financial statement is available upon request to Christian Voice. None of your gift may be deducted under Federal and State income tax laws. *Florida: A COPY OF THE OFFICIAL REGISTRATION AND FINANCIAL INFORMATION MAY BE OBTAINED FROM THE DIVISION OF CONSUMER SERVICES BY CALLING TOLL FREE WITHIN THE STATE, 1-800-435-7352. REGISTRATION DOES NOT IMPLY ENDORSEMENT, APPROVAL, OR RECOMMENDATION, BY THE STATE. 100 percent of your gift is received by Christian Voice. *Georgia: Upon request, Christian Voice will provide a full and fair description of this and its other programs, and a financial statement or summary. *Illinois: Contracts and reports regarding Christian Voice are on file with the Illinois Attorney General. *Kansas: Charity's Kansas registration number is K.S.A.17-17159. The annual financial report for the preceding fiscal year is on file with the Secretary of State. *Minnesota: Zero percent of your gift may be deducted as a charitable contribution under Federal and State income tax laws. *Mississippi: The official registration and financial information of Christian Voice may be obtained from the Mississippi Secretary of State's office by calling 1-888-236-6167. Registration by the Secretary of State does not imply endorsement by the Secretary of State. *New Jersey: INFORMATION FILED WITH THE ATTORNEY GENERAL CONCERNING THIS CHARITABLE SOLICITATION MAY BE OBTAINED FROM THE ATTORNEY GENERAL OF THE STATE OF NEW JERSEY BY CALLING (973) 504-6215. REGISTRATION WITH THE ATTORNEY GENERAL DOES NOT IMPLY ENDORSEMENT. *New York: Upon request, a copy of Christian Voice's last annual report filed with the Department of State is available from Christian Voice or the Office of the Attorney General, Charities Bureau, 120 Broadway, New York, NY 10271. *North Carolina: Financial information about this organization and a copy of its license are available from the State Solicitation Licensing Branch at (919) 733-4510. The license is not an endorsement by the State. *Pennsylvania: The official registration and financial information of Christian Voice may be obtained from the Pennsylvania Department of State by calling toll-free within Pennsylvania, 1-800-732-0999. Registration does not imply endorsement. *Virginia: A financial statement is available from the State Division of Consumer Affairs in the Department of Agriculture and Consumer Services upon request. *Washington: The registration statement required by the Charitable Solicitation Act is on file with the Secretary of State. Additional information can be obtained by calling 1-800-332-4483. *West Virginia: West Virginia residents may obtain a summary of the registration and financial documents from the Secretary of State, State Capitol, Charleston, West Virginia 25305. Registration does not imply endorsement.

Special Discounts Available for Religious and other Nonprofit Groups

Christian Voice is happy to share its 25 years of experience as the pioneer of modern religious activism with religious and civic organizations across the nation. So we are offering a special discount on bulk orders by churches, ministries, service clubs and other nonprofit groups. The grassroots lobbying techniques in this book will help your congregation or membership wield more influence on policymakers and make a difference in America's moral direction.